S0-AYO-764

CONELY BRANCH LIBRARY
4600 MARTIN
DETROIT, MI 48210
(313) 224-6461

JAN '09

APR - - 2001

The Wonder of
SHARKS

To Joel Krauska and G. E. Smith and all kids who love sharks.
— Patricia Corrigan

For a free color catalog describing Gareth Stevens Publishing's list of high-quality books and multimedia programs, call 1-800-542-2595 (USA) or 1-800-461-9120 (Canada). Gareth Stevens Publishing's Fax: (414) 332-3567.

Library of Congress Cataloging-in-Publication Data available upon request from publisher. Fax: (414) 332-3567 for the attention of the Publishing Records Department.

ISBN 0-8368-2665-5

First published in North America in 2000 by
Gareth Stevens Publishing
A World Almanac Education Group Company
330 West Olive Street, Suite 100
Milwaukee, WI 53212 USA

This edition is based on the book *Sharks for Kids* © 1995 by Patricia Corrigan, with illustrations by John F. McGee, first published in the United States in 1995 by NorthWord Press, Inc., Minocqua, Wisconsin, and published as *Shark Magic for Kids* in a library edition by Gareth Stevens, Inc., in 1996. All photographs © 1995 by Pacific Stock, except Bill Curtsinger, 11, 34. Additional end matter © 2000 by Gareth Stevens, Inc.

All rights to this edition reserved to Gareth Stevens, Inc. No part of this book may be reproduced, stored in a retrieval system, or transmitted in any form or by any means, electronic, mechanical, photocopying, recording, or otherwise without the prior written permission of the publisher except for the inclusion of brief quotations in an acknowledged review.

Printed in the United States of America

1 2 3 4 5 6 7 8 9 04 03 02 01 00

APR -- 2001

The Wonder of
SHARKS

by Amy Bauman and Patricia Corrigan
Illustrations by John F. McGee

Gareth Stevens Publishing
A WORLD ALMANAC EDUCATION GROUP COMPANY

Sharks are ancient animals. They first swam the oceans more than 300 million years ago. Sharks lived on Earth even before the first dinosaurs appeared.

Sharks still live in oceans all over the world — but you probably won't see one when you go swimming!

Sharks are fish that live mainly in warm saltwater, but some like cool freshwater. Sharks can be less than 1 foot (0.3 meters) long, but most sharks are longer. Some sharks are *much* longer!

SHARK 3FT - O - 4FT METER 5FT 6FT

7

blue shark

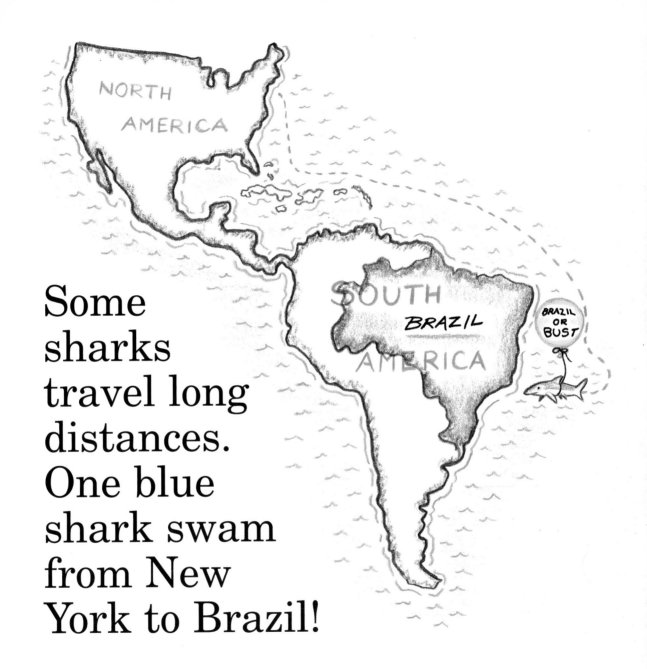

Some sharks travel long distances. One blue shark swam from New York to Brazil!

Most sharks are carnivores, or meat-eaters.

whale shark

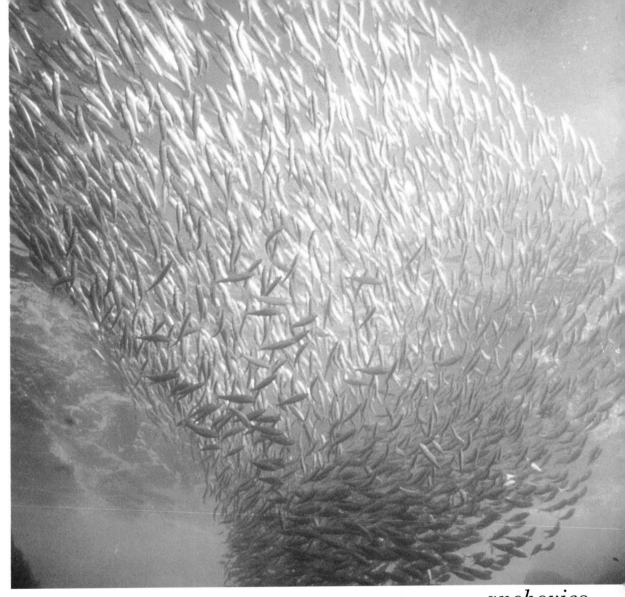

anchovies

They usually eat squid, shellfish, and other fish.

All sharks have several rows of teeth that grow constantly. As their front teeth fall out, their back teeth move forward. A shark can lose 30,000 teeth in its lifetime. Wouldn't that keep a tooth fairy busy?

great white shark

Different types of sharks
have different types of teeth.
The sixgill shark has teeth
that look like little saws.
The night shark has tall,
pointed teeth. The whitetip
shark has triangle-shaped
teeth with sharp edges.

hammerhead shark

Different types of sharks also look different from each other. The hammerhead shark looks like — a hammer!

Hammerhead sharks seem to see and smell better than most other sharks. They can find their favorite food, the stingray, even when it is buried in sand.

Sharks are different from other fish in many ways. For example, the skeletons of most fish are made of bones. The skeletons of sharks are made of tough tissue called cartilage.

whale shark

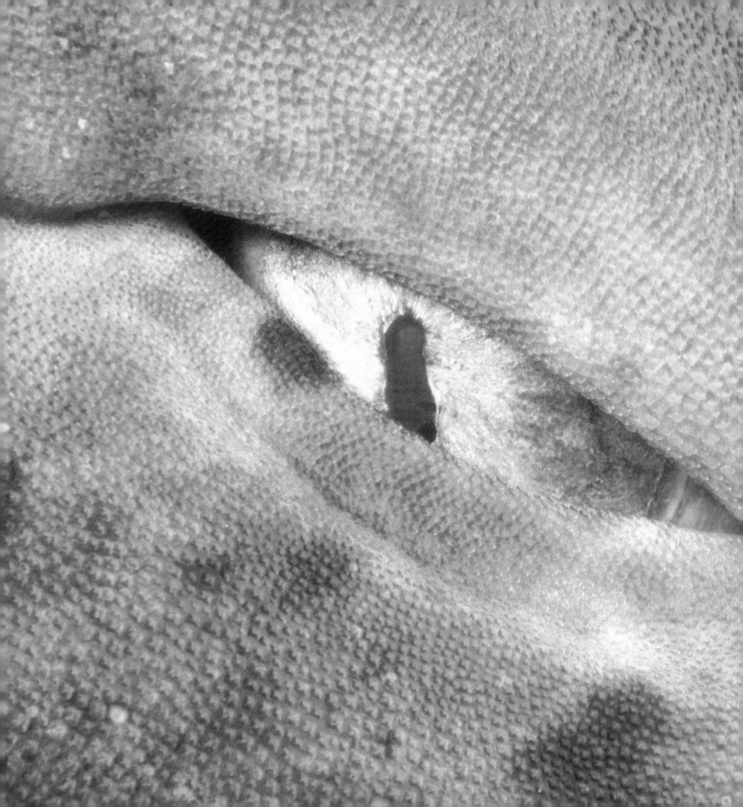

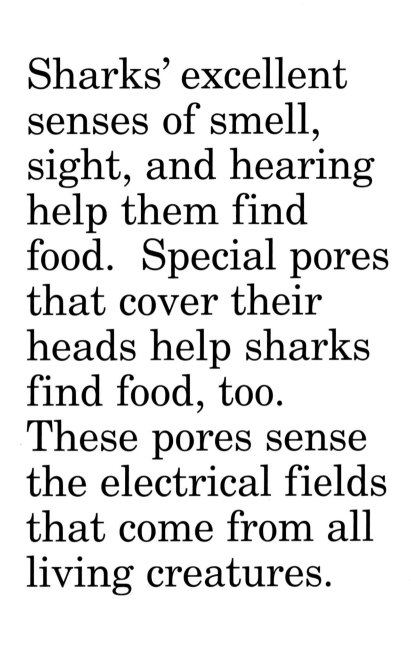

Sharks' excellent senses of smell, sight, and hearing help them find food. Special pores that cover their heads help sharks find food, too. These pores sense the electrical fields that come from all living creatures.

eye of a nurse shark

Most fish lay eggs, but most sharks give birth to live babies called pups. Some sharks lay eggs inside egg cases, which look like leather pouches on the ocean floor. When the pups are born, they break out of the cases.

horn shark

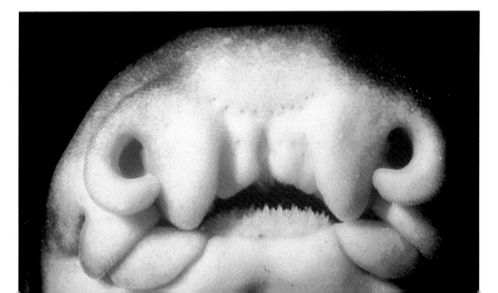

Fish have one gill opening on each side of their heads. Sharks can have as many as seven gill openings. When sharks breathe, they get oxygen from the water that passes through their gills.

nurse shark

25

Scientists believe there are more than 350 species, or types, of sharks. Some shark names, such as cow shark, zebra shark, and elephant shark, seem to have been borrowed from other animals. Other names describe what the sharks look like.

ELE

One shark, called the
nervous shark, is said to
hide its eyes with its tail
when it is caught!

swell shark

Swell sharks "swell up" with water to scare away enemies.

The great white shark is the fiercest of all sharks.

great white shark

shark teeth: ancient (black), today (white)

One of its ancient relatives
had huge teeth.

The biggest shark alive today is the whale shark. It can grow to more than 50 feet (15 m) long and can weigh 40 tons (36 metric tons). The whale shark is the largest fish on Earth.

whale shark

Whale sharks eat krill and plankton. Sometimes, however, they will eat anything they find in the sea — even boots, buckets, and boat oars!

krill

The smallest known shark is the dwarf dogshark, which grows to only about 6.5 inches (16.5 centimeters) long.

Cigar sharks are just a little longer than dwarf dogsharks. These sharks really look a lot like cigars swimming through water!

The nurse shark is a medium-sized shark. It grows to about 9 feet (3 m) long. In some parts of the world, people hunt nurse sharks. Some hunt them for food. Others hunt them for their thick skin, which is used to make leather for shoes.

Shark skin is very tough and can feel like sandpaper. It is covered with little, toothlike scales called denticles. As sharks grow, they shed the denticles and grow new, larger ones.

great white shark

Sharks are very strong, quick animals. They can swim as fast as 40 miles (64 kilometers) an hour.

Many people believe that sharks attack humans, but most shark species do not.

great white shark

Even for dangerous species, people are not a favorite food. Sharks would rather eat other fish, crabs, shrimp, and squid. Some eat larger marine animals. One shark even ate an entire reindeer!

whitetip shark

Often, when people say they don't like sharks or are afraid of sharks, they just don't understand them. Sharks are extremely important to ocean life and play a valuable role in our natural world.

tiger shark

Glossary

ancient – very old

carnivores – animals that eat meat

cartilage – tough, white tissue that forms the skeletons of some animals

electrical fields – areas that contain the electrical charges produced by living creatures. These areas surround the bodies of the creatures.

gill opening – a thin slit leading to an organ that draws oxygen from water

krill – tiny sea creatures eaten by many fish, seabirds, and water mammals

plankton – masses of very tiny plant and animal life found in water

pores – small openings in the skin of an animal or plant

pups – the young of certain animals, such as sharks, seals, and dogs

Index